WOLF TAIL GLIMMER

WOLF TAIL GLIMMER

Bedell Phillips

Wolf Tail Glimmer
©2019 by Bedell Phillips

ISBN#: 978-1-950381-20-3

Published by Piscataqua Press
An imprint of RiverRun Bookstore
32 Daniel St., Portsmouth NH 03801
www.ppressbooks.com

Printed in the United States of America
using the font New Aster

For my mother

Poet's Notes

I do write some poetry that calls for a traditional format, including the narrative. However, for several years the sound of the word thrum has affected my work, evoking the respite of gently moving water or the shock of electrocution. Merriam-Webster defines the word thrum as "threads left on the loom after the cloth has been removed." Some of these threads are longer and some are shorter. As I live long, I realize what is important in life are the little things. To emphasize this phenomenon I have invented the poetry Thrum©. Some of my Thrums are couplets, tercets, even quatrains. All have a characteristic final line. This brings the reader the zap, the crux, or the essence, why I write.

Table of Contents

Perpetual

in the middle of Great Bay
the lightest puddle, water smooth and blue

shore marked with reclining long clean
tree trunks washed by brackish water

he, solitary proud undisturbed
without movement, a loon

as 160 million years ago

Adagio
  relaxed speed of a musical work

storm colors density of soft grey owl feathers
hard shale and dark charcoal

cloud burst downpour
storm room compacted showers

pointillist water drops
onto the slate channel

sometime soothing

Random Good Idea

while researching in his lab
Einstein watched pollen in water

led him to the atom

White Juvenile

drab feathers insignificant display speckled
body protects baby through first spring

pale green lore between his eyes and beak
matches the legs, toes grabbing jetty rocks

moves with care fighting a fall, quick jettison
no longer dreary his underside pure white

small dark wingtips dazzle against the sky

In the Heat

standing naked
watch the rainfall

rust never sleeps
hope steals through the night

Tree Trunk Picket Fence

autumn in New Hampshire
red pines lichen encrusted

wolf tail glimmer
between the trees

light dances on
the trunk fungus

you can never know

An Outdoor Shower

Wash away the sins of the world

falling sun yellows the red pine
needles

in the shower she looks over the
gate

roses done blooming, just nibs and
thorns

the advent of death
dying

ending the quick former voluptuous
life

Gifts

my gift to look
atrocity in the eye and fight

for the little guy
the homeless child

my gift for fixing things
given up for dead

my gift for ardor
relentless despite the powerful

my gift for beauty the simple kind
content with a small bloom

I won't surrender my aura
my orb my chi my esprit

never loveless sometimes alone

Mistake

the dock was
too hot

to get in the water
you had to burn your feet

but the cracks were small
it fell through unnoticed

diamond of hope

Busted

small white boat at mooring 3017 wrapped to the gills
control panel front passenger seats and captain's chair

his plan to keep it spotless enhanced by stern
to bow red and silver metallic streamers

upgraded by five-foot wind spinner
his boat would not be dirty

a cormorant swoops down the estuary
searching for a sunny landing spot

lands on the mooring spreads his wings full
can't fish 'til the wings are dry

hearing *thwa thwa* turns his head
stays a while fascinated by the Bird-b-Gone

at long last he's dried could eat
more takes off over the boat

drops alms for the owner

Study in Autumn

Winslow Homer sky
pumpkin pie

vast rolling field
cut short earth naked
shoots revealed

swath leads to
soft green tootsie rolls
smelling rich and sweet

hay rolls nutrition
barn full of livestock
this winter no starvation

placed mid meadow
disregarded technology
aimless telephone pole

no one knows why it's there
no one gives it thought or cares

Ghoul Colossus

old pole in the middle of a hayfield
bordered by railroad tracks and macadam road

a month ago fertilizing
checked height of rye grass
sufficient growth to bale
tedder spreads hay to dry
hitch up the New Holland rig
adjust the chamber regulator
to the proper round bale size
new mown grass makes
sculpted curved path
exquisite landscape

lonely in its midfield
tied to a telephone pole
two-story high inflatable
black cartoon face
arched eyebrows down turned mouth
whites of his eyes circled in green
matched by bowtie and waistcoat buttons
daunting villainous eyes
dagger toe nails

degradation of our pastoral field

"Iceland" Photograph by Michael Morris 2009

smooth black stucco house
red tin roof two dormer windows
narrow alley with black graffiti
cement sidewalk butts up to the home
thin metal street light arches
above the roof like a flamingo's neck
normal white line street divider impeded
by large chartreuse polka-dot diagonal pattern

macadam artistry marking nothing

Funeral

Odiorne Point rocky shore
pneumonia-inducing drizzle

ironic pure white tent points disrespectfully
at myriad grey stripes in the sky

fog rolls in from Maine coast
empty white chairs folded open for mourners

death in the air

Dead Mouse

floating in the water
long feet splayed behind
winsome whiskers
pointed nose
quiet tiny toes
reeked havoc now motionless

if not for disease, charming

Foundling Dog

touched my hand at the SPCA
chocolate fur through metal cage

triangle black nose skin wet
long curved tail wagging

brought him home up on the couch
so happy he licked my thigh

first time since college boyfriend

Bunny Plague

six-year old says "how can you
kill them they're so cute"

grown son adds "you're a pacifist and
you're offing 'em"

"look, I'd annihilate them if I could
they're eating my tomatoes berries and beans"

"yes" replies the daughter-in-law
"my grandparents raised rabbits as a crop"

American Men Nearly Naked

nearly naked in NH sunrise
hitches up jeans in the autumn woods
behind his motorcycle
upper body green and purple
grungy tattoo mosaics
bend and zip fly
swish and crunch leaves

nearly naked in MD
high noon at the gas station
wearing only shorts
right chest "sweet"
left chest "salty"
in bold gothic tats

woodsmen and show-off
sweet and sour

American yin and yang

60 Year-Old Virgin

he walked through the door tall fit with blue eyes
carrying his bag of tools her lock was rusted she couldn't open the door
her heart palpitated he looked kind she needed her door to work

in the grocery store cuz her heart doctor insisted on coconut milk
it was nowhere to be found her back was hurting that day
standing next to her was a tan short man with his abs showing
through his t-shirt, "you look like you need help" he smiled
she looked down at him, "you look like you play a lot of sports"

on the dock a guy was working on his boat
tiny bathing suit revealed all his butt
thick and round, the ripples on his stomach
were so tight they pulled his navel up into a big dent
they got talking, "wanna go for a coffee?"

she decided against it

Palm Beach Halloween

boob job held up
by black bustier

under a body suit
of flesh tones & bandages

another wearing white
bandeau breasts overflowing

skeleton bones going up
from her feet past cleavage to white face

scary group of bulging ripe cantaloupes

Nice Guy Loser

men's Lily Pulitzer trunks
some yellow lots of peacock
blue upside down sailboats

old and gray at the temples
loved those designer patterns
his oldest Gucci loafers at his feet

perfect nose wrinkled skin
too much time too much sun

loveless despite of all the fun

Unexpected

they were young inexperienced
only an undergraduate degree

the nerve they had to start this
company and play with the big boys

their first healthcare conference
a national one big

he was edgy as they flew
to Sanibel Island in the Gulf of Mexico

naturally he'd been uptight, still
producing 75 hours nonstop

she'd been wanting to escape the marriage
"not on my team" she frequently thought

at last there, she was ready waiting horny
his usual sexual game had been missing

the hotel room expanded
ocean vivid cerulean clear

she opened those lips for him
now he checked in

she moved closer
he was like never before

a long red explosion
in the mystery of her dark center

like their garden's emperor tulip

Heartbreak Hatchet Job

From behind her he said, "Hey look who's here." "You know how I like
to go out." "Yes, first hand," he grinned that charming Irish grin. "Well," she
thought, *I'm not falling for his crap again*. "This place is pretty hot." Now
he leered, "Wild enough for you?" *Shit*. "Actually I'm meeting some
friends." "The more the merrier." Her friends jumped up when the band
started playing "Uptown Funk" a Bruno Mars rap. Belting it out, table-
danced, "gon' give it to you". The white female lead in a crotch-short
gold shimmy, feral fat electric guitarist shod in socks, chic all-black sax
except his white chest-pieces tie. Jumping to the beat with her friends but
still obsessed with Irish. So much intense dating, then nothing. Six months
thinking of him daily, making up conversations. Ghosted. Baudelaire's
Kisses as icy as the moon.

L'Hôtel Les Bains

Princess Caroline of Monaco, drag queens, black kids from the projects that
got in cuz they dressed wicked cool, suburbanites who took the train into
Paris, all had a hoot. Combined in a mélée, radical artists, intellectuals, 18
and 70 year-olds. Warhol would take the Concorde three-hour flight from
New York, eat, then hit Les Bains to party. Fly back to New York the next
day with no jet lag. Now filled with avant-garde art, king-sized beds,
condoms in every room. Rich techie kids, wealthy businessmen, and
American tourists revere its history, relish the rowdiness.

A Moment in Paris

In 1885 Les Bains began giving Japanese, Russian, and Turkish sulfur baths.
Proust, a regular, took steam, workers from les Halles (the stomach of Paris)
came before dawn for a shower and café calva. During 1978, two friends
rented it, decided to make it into a rock concert hall, then a night club,
restaurant, and bar. Depeche Mode, Simple Minds, and famous personalities
followed: Keith Harding, Andy Warhol, Basquiat, Yves Saint Laurent,
Robert De Niro, Catherine Deneuve, Spike Lee, Kim Basinger, David
Bowie, Mick Jagger. Kate Moss had her 25th birthday party there. By 2010,
it needed extreme rehab. The lengthy Paris permit process enabled a
months-long radical art event. This collective place of music, dance, and
misbehaving then became a chic boutique hotel. I stayed there and met
Fahim, son of a Saudi sheik. We went together on les Bateaux Mouches
night boat cruise up the Seine. On the way back to the dock, we heard yelled
from an overhead bridge *in English*, "I love you."

Happenstance

He had quite a cough
She was worried about the cab home
He carried a knapsack
She had a tiny chic bag
He listened quietly to the menu
She asked questions
Small restaurant they were seated close
He carefully picked at his salad plate
She noticed the wall was covered with artist's writings
He tried not to look at her
The main course came, she said "the fish has bones"
He neatly pulled the bones off his fish
She read the wall from top to bottom
He looked at the walls with a glance, foreign gibberish
They both ordered floating island for dessert
He was in Paris for five days
She got there a day before him
He was going home to Australia
She lived in Ireland
He wants to grab her for the rest of his life

Wrong John

they didn't know each other well
went dancing anyway

with internet dating
that's just the way it is

his wife died two years ago, his date in a sundress
no underwear hadn't had sex in three months

the band was hot
the weather humid

Bobby Joe left to get another scotch
Shania didn't care checked out hot dance-floor men

hispanic guy moving his hand up from
his date's butt towards her slut top

when Bobby Joe came back
she said I have to go to the pot

the john door was blocked by confusing rows
of see-through bamboo stalks

about to piss on her leg she leapt
towards the bathroom opening

just tripped forward breasts flopping
stopped her fall grabbing the wall

above the urinal in full sight a penis held fully erect

Dinner and Dancing

Eating outdoors as usual in Florida. This time the old guy picked her up at
the condo. When he got out of his showy convertible, she did the fat-pot
scan. No result. Could he be fit? He wore his yellow polo shirt fancy belt
navy Bermudas and sneaks, very non-old fart. She had skinny jeans and a
tight purple jersey down to her hips. "Wanna go dancing next door?"
"Sure" he answered quickly. He knew a sneakily convenient place to park.
They walked down a dark lane to the rowdy bar. Next to the road a guy
was sniffing something in a car with barely any paint. She felt oddly safe
along side her date. As they got close the music blared. "It'll be okay if
it's not country" she smiled. The band was hot, five pieces two guitars.
40 year-olds stood around watched at first. She looked over. He was tense
tight-lipped but his right foot was tapping to the music. Later everyone
was doing the bump n' grind. Of course she joined in, then shook her
booty. He got a hard-on right then. *Whew* she thought *it still works.*

Internet Dating

his username was artisan
he'd finished college showed a headshot
and was nearby

funny how few standards you develop

he didn't want to spend time
tired of months chatting on the web
asked if they could talk and gave her his phone

sounds like a good idea

there was a cool place
with cheap food
and wild dance music

how bad could it be

she got there first
was chatting with the waitress
told them she was waiting on an internet date

they laughed hysterically at the idea

"see that guy far across the parking
lot the one wearing pink
he could be nice"

across the sidewalk he limped old fat and pimply

Condo Nazi

Longwood Gardens
leading horticulturist

falls in love with his job
because one night

while alone far out on the pond
a single night-blooming cereus

shines white in
midnight light

scary news about his Mom
flies down straight away

condo plants by the elevator
limp dry and dying

instinct moves him
to save them by watering

from nowhere
a hidden voice screams

"Don't you touch that plant"

Serendipity

when he came back to his old house
all seemed in order as he went

through the refrigerator did a random check
pulled out the bottom crisper

found a dark hole
in the floor of the appliance

upon close inspection
it had teeth marks bitten

through the floor
looking on the inside door

his bag of gluten free
flour was also gnawed

shitfaced he walked out front
across the street a large white truck

with the bold blue letters
appliance services

"hi there do you repair refrigerators?"
"yes of course"

back in the house the man
checked it out

he went back to his truck
returned with steel wool and metallic tape

bent over and
covered the hole

astonished the homeowner
blurted "god I really owe you"

"oh its nothing
just give me twenty bucks"

Neem

India religious phenomenon
widows thrown on funeral pyres
nude religious men

Khajuraho bas-relief
deviant forms of sex but
educated women playing the sitar

the bus group was tired napping
but sharp over the loudspeaker "we have
special arrangement, barbeque"

tourists overwhelmed by the train ride with
armless legless multiple forms of crippled
malnourished children dark blank yearning eyes

at long last the travelers freed, sat under
the seven-branched Neem tree
thick dark bark

clear sky, while they eat tikka masala
disease forgotten
relieved by honey-sweet earth

India's intensity assuaged

On the Water

Looking at a view from the terrazza surrounded by water and gondolas. Through the limestone trefoils many dudes are poling by. In traditional gondolier hats others with baseball caps occasionally bareheaded. Dark Italian mop of hair, a blonde with tats, all fit and hot. Always dressed in dark pants, black and white striped short-sleeved shirts. Many wearing sneaks, one guy with a sock on one foot and barefoot on the other. Balance is needed.

On the solarai, where the gondolier stands, there is an enameled wood stern with a crummy mat or even an oriental rug bolted onto the deck. Varying sculpture figures, including a gold Neptune holding a trident. Bow to stern all black, some flat, some gloss, some raised patterns: acanthus, filigree.

Midship: assorted damask furniture, always a two-person couch, two stools and a chair sometimes spindled, sometimes a rounded splat. Always with only one arm to help tourists depart given unstable water. A pair of seahorses with curly tails, symbols of protection.

The tip of the bow, to balance the weight of the gondolier, has a large silver ferro. Top rounded, an homage to the Rialto Bridge. Beneath, a six-tooth comb representing the many Venetian islands, including Murano. Long pointed bow ends with a frieze: plain, raised filigree, or an oil painting.

In embedded silver lies a plaque dedicating the boat to: Lucia, a mother; Alessandro, a brother; or senza nome, no name, the girlfriend that left him.

She Got Up

eight years old and short
she'd never done it before

they went out to Lake Spofford
Kathy's dad had a new boat

"we're gonna go water skiing" her friend
asked "it's so fun have you done it?"

Molly had to say, "no
is it scary?"

"nope, you'll see
the lake is real fun"

hours later Molly's still in the water
Kathy was shouting "you can do it"

"aah Mr. Heneage, I've tried 14 times
I don't think I can get up"

"you know honey, I love driving my new boat
I'll do this till its dark"

"OK I'm ready." the little blond head
rose through the troth of water

she got up stood tall
"Molly I knew you would make it"

Mr. Heneage is wicked cool

Granddaughter and her Grampy

sitting at the table after Thanksgiving
he said "Do we have any Coke?"

she answered "Yes in the fridge"
together they gulped it all down

"You know you can smash it"
she looked at those fine blue eyes

"Want me to show you?"
"I can't do it"

"Oh yes you can   watch," Grampy
punched his forehead   with the can

she believed him took a deep breath
crushed the can   didn't even hurt

it was easy

Encounter

cold Pennsylvania
morning very early

her mom's bed all fluffy
under pure white comforter

kindergartener ventured
in "Mom it's 8:02"

"Huh ahh get cereal" mom had
corrected college papers all night

"I'll be with you soon
and give you a kiss"

"Mom, it's 8:30 now I have
to go the bus is here

and I know you lied to me again."

Sparky's

Her grandmother hugged her. "We have to go to Burlington. Uncle Wendel's a star. He doesn't drink anymore."

She loved him. Sometimes when Mom worked, she'd go to his place after school. With light in his eyes, he'd say, "Can you keep a secret?" Honored, she answered, "Yes I can." They'd walk down his road to Sparky's Bar.

"You can't ever tell." "I never tell," she promised with her heart. The place was warm, smelled funny. Wendel in his lowest voice asked her, "And what's your job?" "I know, I know," she said, "to watch the clock for 5, then we go home."

Now Wendel speaks all over the country, sober for 44 years.

Abner

our own black
and white
cat lost
but dad
has no tears
hunt through
the cinder blocks
wall into pines' darkness

dad repined
owning his regret
I look out the window
neglect's revenge
his trespass fells
the silver oak's crown

this monster has no breath

Sideswiped

parked her car in front of the police station
lot was packed, towering black trucks
minute slots between parking spaces
flashing cruisers, rowdy teens, noisy suspects

before she could look a giant SUV crunched
her convertible, smashed right next to her head
fancy lady space cadet gets out of her car
cop says "stay where you are we'll get a tow truck"

Ford 8-wheeler rig
210 horsepower engine 1200 torque
young driver green reflective vest
black hat and t-shirt jumps out

"how'd she crash you?"
"no idea bore into me like a tidal wave"
"might be safer if you get in my truck"
the victim lunged up to the seat

coffee cup covered floor three staplers
well greased grim black interior
filth blanketed floor

rescuer's face unshaven stubble grimy hands
fingernail grunge ruptured cuticle
tat of Mickey Mouse getting the finger

she watched while he smoothly loaded the car, blurted
"this is appalling right in front of all the cops"

"That's nothing, Miss. I'm usually here three times a week"

Near Death Experience

she had to go over to the hospital
across the street in downtown Philly

they were on deadline
a problem with the CEO's message

her boss was shit-faced
gave her no address

stepping off the curb
nasty invisible cab

her nerves splintered
blaring bus horns

high-rise complex panic
she couldn't find the building

in a warren of narrow corridors
lying on a gurney gray gaunt body

hand off the litter with a sore, an inch from her

Former Lover

met him on the 4th of July
at the Boston Esplanade Concert

a friend introduced them
tall kind and an architect

on the first date she wore
a sequined bandeau top

and no underwear
with high hopes

saw him years later
sitting on his front stoop

next to his old buddy
and the fuzzy dog

"he talks about you a lot
in his Alzheimer's rants"

she smelled that sweet lilac tree
just like the old days looking into

his same true clear eyes but he wasn't there

In the News

Antarctica—

Births to breeding pairs of Chin Strap Penguins known to return
to the same mate year after year, declined by 40% as rising
temperatures create a rapid loss of krill–their main food source.

Mauritania—

Recurrent extreme drought has caused winds to sweep over
previously arable land in the seaside city Nouakchott. Sand dunes
cover roads, demolish homes. The country suffers from chronic food
insecurity.

Lake Tai—

Around Shanghai, Suzhou and Changzhou lies China's third largest
lake. These cities' fast growth created sewer dumping, changes in
agriculture and drainage from livestock. Resulting algae blooms gave
two million people pea soup slime coming through their faucets. The
government had to bring in clean water.

Chicago—

January 30, 2019 temperatures 45 below zero, coldest in 150 years.

One World Trade Center

largest bunker in the world withstands
violent natural phenomenon

demonic terrorist intent and explosions
with cutting edge anti-terror life support

rises from the old site today on the northwest corner
16 acre world trade center site 1776 foot-high monument

cement base engineered beams and cables
concrete equivalent to two Empire State buildings

skyscraper glass panels floor to ceiling
1200 pounds each sealed into the concrete base

best construction workers rise
from lobby to the top in one-minute elevators

third generation ironworker supervisor cleared the wreckage of 9/11
men worked 6 winters on the job in subzero temperature

even if two columns fail the high-technology
materials mix ensures the building still stands

magnific symbol of American resurrection

American Political Process

second president to promote an accused
female abuser supreme court justice

85% of female republicans believe Justice Kavanaugh
is innocent according to credible sources

fifteen year old girl came to a house after a club party gathering one guy
shoved her next a seventeen year old future justice attacked her in the
bedroom

promotion of white male power allowed dismissal
of one more woman's testimony as to actual events

Susan Collins Maine Senator
casts the swing vote

harm from females within   harm from without

Offense

old white-boy executive
anxious to date called three times in one week

"I wanna get laid" he said in the car
hurt, repulsed, revolted

his date said "you disrespect me
women's rights and the Constitution

you're without couth make my flesh crawl"

An Odd Parallel

the western India purple frog
lives in slime crawls
out once a year to procreate

you Mr. President
also live in the slime
crawl out just for a fuck

immune venal untouchable

Softness of Fiddler's Tones

Trump country in a small log cabin planked wooden
ceiling soft beige curtains hung from solid wood rods
a godly older couple insurance guy young white man with two black
kids many grandmothers and young musicians all singing in unison
hymn #8 *Leaning leaning, safe and secure from all alarms,*
I'm leaning on the everlasting arms

a sweet grey-haired man in ukulele shirt strums his banjo
butch cut honey-haired woman in short shorts plays a silver flute
bleached blonde heavy mascaraed bombshell mouths her harmonica
unshaven threadbare dude on hootin' mandolin decorated with Apple
stickers church lady rocking out on her colossal blue enameled guitar
six other random guitars bringing down the house

during the break they eat at the kitchen bar Kroger's cupcakes coffee-
mate container of juice cut fruit cheese Ritz crackers box of cookies
required glass of plastic forks paper plates and a donation basket

America united

Ties That Bind

in a small village by the bandstand
traffic clogged street

done with black trucks flying American
flags and Trump signs taped to the bed

another damn pick-up boor honking
she looks the other way

third honk she opens her car door
stomps out "dear Christ"

found a small beige wallet she left
on the trunk at the gas station

hater rescued

Ataraxia

άταραξία: state of ongoing freedom from distress
and worry–Epicurus

one day is a long time with you
one day brings too many thoughts

lost in the city I ran behind your car
didn't bother to look in your rear view

turned the corner out of sight
gave me no thought no directions home--

garrotes sanity
poisons marrow

decimates the jugular
slaughters the formerly free

I refuse this fight I search for the tranquil

Taken

through my gate
past the Adirondack chair

a Little Blue Heron
struts across the porch

hunts then dives
through the crown of thorns

grabs a chameleon stands back her nose
and tail hangs out of his mouth

two shakes of his head
swallows her whole

failed camouflage

"Out my back door"
Crosby, Stills, and Nash

Polaris near earth's celestial pole
shines nightly in the Little Dipper giving direction

her brother diagnosed with rare blood cancer
other brother committed suicide

flights to the hospital sterile room
funeral arrangements death details

but Jupiter, God of Luck rising in the east

Rufous Hummingbird

in Utah for the summer
parents desert babies

as days shorten
kids feel the need to fly

travel through night
darkness avoids predators

instinct teaches every stop-over
exact arrival at parents' destination

longest migration per inch of
body length for all species

soft rouge throat settles on my porch

Coriolis Effect
quest for love

ever present search
as relentless water surges
from Europe to Newfoundland
Morocco to the Carolinas

lovers watch seaside tide
colors come in some
bright shining stones
some dark

tide ebbs exposing
threats beneath
barnacles Portuguese
Man-of-War

explosive organic
flowing in and out
rapid than quiet

washed out tumult
relief rested replete
mien serene

decrescendo

Acknowledgements

All gratitude to: the Palm Beach Poetry Festival and particularly Chard deNiord, Tom Sleigh, and Rodney Jones. The author gratefully acknowledges: the nomination for *Best of the Net* by *Gravel Magazine,* University of Arkansas, June issue, 2013: "Thinking about the Violence"; *Gravel:* "Good Night Irene," and "The Near Convert"; *FFUSE*: "Cullen"; *The Big Windows Writing Review*, Writing Center at Washtenaw, Ann Arbor, MI, Issue 11, Spring 2018: "Eclipsing the Grave." My deep thanks to my interns, my readers, and my mentor, Tom Lux.